THE SYMPHONY OF STARS

CONTEMPORARY ROMANCE WITH MAGICAL REALISM

Chapter 1: The Unexpected Encounter

ELLA HARPER ENTERED THE BOOKSTORE WITH A SIGH OF RELIEF. THE COOL, AIR-CONDITIONED ATMOSPHERE WAS A WELCOME ESCAPE FROM THE SWELTERING COASTAL HEAT. THE BOOKSTORE, PAGES AND MEMORIES, WAS A HAVEN OF CALM, WITH ITS WOODEN SHELVES CRAMMED FULL OF BOOKS AND THE FAINT SCENT OF AGED PAPER. ELLA HAD RECENTLY RELOCATED TO THIS SMALL TOWN, SEEKING SOLACE AND A FRESH START AFTER A PAINFUL PAST.

AS SHE WANDERED THROUGH THE AISLES, HER FINGERS LIGHTLY TRACED THE SPINES OF BOOKS. HER THOUGHTS WERE INTERRUPTED WHEN A VOICE BEHIND HER SAID, "LOOKING FOR SOMETHING SPECIFIC?"

ELLA TURNED TO SEE A MAN WITH A WARM SMILE AND TWINKLING EYES. HE HAD AN EASY CHARM ABOUT HIM, WITH TOUSLED BROWN HAIR AND A HINT OF MISCHIEF. HE INTRODUCED HIMSELF AS LUCAS BENNETT, AN AUTHOR WHO FREQUENTED THE STORE. HE NOTICED HER INTEREST IN A RARE BOOK ON THE TOP SHELF AND OFFERED TO HELP.
"DO YOU COME HERE OFTEN?" ELLA ASKED, TRYING TO SOUND CASUAL.

"WHENEVER I NEED INSPIRATION OR JUST A GOOD ESCAPE FROM REALITY," LUCAS REPLIED. HE EFFORTLESSLY RETRIEVED THE BOOK FOR HER. "I'M LUCAS, BY THE WAY. AND YOU ARE?" "ELLA," SHE RESPONDED, FEELING AN UNEXPECTED FLUTTER OF NERVES. "JUST MOVED HERE, TRYING TO FIND SOME PEACE."

LUCAS'S EYES SOFTENED. "WELL, I'M SURE THIS TOWN HAS A LOT TO OFFER. IT'S QUIET BUT FULL OF SURPRISES."
THEIR BRIEF CONVERSATION LEFT ELLA INTRIGUED. AS SHE LEFT THE BOOKSTORE, SHE COULDN'T HELP BUT WONDER ABOUT THE ENIGMATIC MAN WHO SEEMED TO UNDERSTAND HER NEED FOR A FRESH START.

Chapter 2: The Melancholic Melody ♡

ELLA'S APARTMENT WAS A JUMBLE OF MOVING BOXES AND SCATTERED SHEET MUSIC. SHE HAD HOPED THE CHANGE OF SCENERY WOULD REIGNITE HER PASSION FOR THE VIOLIN, BUT SO FAR, THE MELODIES ELUDED HER. HER ONLY COMPANY WAS THE MUSIC THAT FILLED THE ROOM, BUT IT SEEMED TO MOCK HER FRUSTRATION.

THAT EVENING, LUCAS INVITED ELLA TO A SMALL LITERARY GATHERING AT AN OLD, CHARMING THEATER. ELLA HESITATED BUT DECIDED TO GO. THE THEATER WAS INTIMATE, ITS VINTAGE DECOR AND SOFT LIGHTING CREATING AN INVITING ATMOSPHERE. LUCAS WAS READING EXCERPTS FROM HIS LATEST NOVEL, AND ELLA WAS CAPTIVATED BY THE DEPTH AND EMOTION IN HIS WORDS.

AFTER THE READING, LUCAS APPROACHED HER. "HOW WAS THAT? I HOPE YOU ENJOYED IT."
"IT WAS BEAUTIFUL," ELLA SAID SINCERELY. "I FELT... INSPIRED." LUCAS SMILED. "I'M GLAD TO HEAR THAT. YOUR PRESENCE ADDED SOMETHING SPECIAL TO THE EVENING."

LATER, AS THEY WALKED THROUGH THE QUIET STREETS, ELLA COULDN'T SHAKE THE FEELING THAT LUCAS'S WORDS HAD TOUCHED SOMETHING DEEP WITHIN HER. SHE FELT A RENEWED SENSE OF PURPOSE, AND FOR THE FIRST TIME IN A LONG WHILE, THE MELODIES BEGAN TO STIR WITHIN HER.

Chapter 3:
Echoes of the Past

LUCAS VISITS ELLA'S APARTMENT WITH PASTRIES. THEY CHAT ABOUT THEIR CREATIVE PROCESSES AND PERSONAL EXPERIENCES. ELLA IS TOUCHED BY HIS THOUGHTFULNESS. LUCAS SUGGESTS ELLA BLEND HER PERSONAL EXPERIENCES WITH HER MUSIC, SPARKING A NEW IDEA IN HER.

THEY TAKE A STROLL IN THE RAIN, WHICH ADDS A MAGICAL QUALITY TO THEIR INTERACTION. LUCAS SHARES LOCAL LEGENDS AND STORIES, DEEPENING THEIR CONNECTION. THE RAIN-WASHED STREETS AND HEARTFELT CONVERSATION LEAD TO A DEEPER UNDERSTANDING BETWEEN ELLA AND LUCAS.

IMPACT ON ELLA:
BACK AT HOME,
ELLA PRACTICES
HER VIOLIN
WITH A NEW
PERSPECTIVE.
THE
COMBINATION
OF LUCAS'S
INSIGHTS AND
THEIR SHARED
MOMENTS HELP
HER FIND NEW
INSPIRATION.

Chapter 4: A New Harmony ♡

ELLA EXPERIMENTS WITH INTEGRATING HER PERSONAL EXPERIENCES INTO HER MUSIC. HER COMPOSITIONS REFLECT HER EVOLVING EMOTIONAL STATE AND GROWING CONNECTION TO THE TOWN. LUCAS CONTINUES TO SUPPORT ELLA, AND THEY SPEND MORE TIME TOGETHER EXPLORING THE TOWN AND SHARING THEIR PASSIONS.

THEIR FRIENDSHIP
GROWS STRONGER
AS THEY BOND OVER
THEIR MUTUAL LOVE
FOR CREATIVITY.
ELLA BEGINS TO
FEEL MORE AT HOME
IN THE TOWN.
ELLA STARTS TO SEE
THE TOWN AS A
PLACE OF
POTENTIAL AND
GROWTH, RATHER
THAN JUST A
TEMPORARY REFUGE.

ELLA'S MUSIC BEGINS TO RESONATE WITH THE COMMUNITY, MARKING THE BEGINNING OF HER INTEGRATION INTO THE LOCAL SCENE. LUCAS'S PRESENCE REMAINS A SIGNIFICANT SOURCE OF SUPPORT.

Chapter 5: The Tapestry of Memories

ELLA PERFORMS AT A LOCAL EVENT, SHOWCASING HER NEW COMPOSITIONS. THE PERFORMANCE IS WELL-RECEIVED, AND ELLA FEELS A DEEP SENSE OF ACCOMPLISHMENT. LUCAS AND ELLA SHARE A MOMENT OF CELEBRATION AND REFLECTION AFTER THE PERFORMANCE, ACKNOWLEDGING THEIR PERSONAL GROWTH.

ELLA REFLECTS ON HOW FAR SHE HAS COME SINCE MOVING TO THE TOWN. HER MUSIC NOW CARRIES A DEEPER EMOTIONAL RESONANCE, THANKS TO HER EXPERIENCES AND LUCAS'S INFLUENCE.
ELLA AND LUCAS'S BOND STRENGTHENS AS THEY SUPPORT EACH OTHER IN THEIR RESPECTIVE CREATIVE ENDEAVORS.

ELLA STARTS TO ENVISION HER FUTURE IN THE TOWN, FEELING MORE HOPEFUL AND CONFIDENT ABOUT HER PATH FORWARD. THE SUPPORT AND CONNECTION WITH LUCAS PLAY A CRUCIAL ROLE IN HER JOURNEY.

Chapter 5: The Tapestry of Memories

ELLA PERFORMS AT A LOCAL EVENT, SHOWCASING HER NEW COMPOSITIONS. THE PERFORMANCE IS WELL-RECEIVED, AND ELLA FEELS A DEEP SENSE OF ACCOMPLISHMENT. LUCAS AND ELLA SHARE A MOMENT OF CELEBRATION AND REFLECTION AFTER THE PERFORMANCE, ACKNOWLEDGING THEIR PERSONAL GROWTH.

ELLA REFLECTS ON HOW FAR SHE HAS COME SINCE MOVING TO THE TOWN. HER MUSIC NOW CARRIES A DEEPER EMOTIONAL RESONANCE, THANKS TO HER EXPERIENCES AND LUCAS'S INFLUENCE.
ELLA AND LUCAS'S BOND STRENGTHENS AS THEY SUPPORT EACH OTHER IN THEIR RESPECTIVE CREATIVE ENDEAVORS.

ELLA STARTS TO ENVISION HER FUTURE IN THE TOWN, FEELING MORE HOPEFUL AND CONFIDENT ABOUT HER PATH FORWARD. THE SUPPORT AND CONNECTION WITH LUCAS PLAY A CRUCIAL ROLE IN HER JOURNEY.

Chapter 6: The Unveiling ♡

ELLA DECIDES TO CONFRONT UNRESOLVED ISSUES FROM HER PAST, WITH LUCAS'S SUPPORT. THEY REVISIT OLD MEMORIES AND PLACES SIGNIFICANT TO HER. LUCAS SHARES A PERSONAL REVELATION, DEEPENING THEIR RELATIONSHIP AND ADDING COMPLEXITY TO THEIR CONNECTION.

THE EXPLORATION
OF THEIR PASTS
BECOMES A JOURNEY
OF SELF-DISCOVERY
AND MUTUAL
UNDERSTANDING.
THEY SUPPORT EACH
OTHER THROUGH
EMOTIONAL
MOMENTS.
ELLA AND LUCAS
GROW CLOSER AS
THEY FACE THEIR
FEARS AND
UNCERTAINTIES
TOGETHER.

THE SHARED
EXPERIENCES
STRENGTHEN
THEIR BOND AND
SET THE STAGE
FOR A DEEPER
RELATIONSHIP.
ELLA FEELS A
RENEWED SENSE
OF CLARITY AND
PURPOSE.

Chapter 7: The Convergence ♡

ELLA AND LUCAS BEGIN A COLLABORATIVE PROJECT THAT BLENDS HIS WRITING WITH HER MUSIC. THEY FACE CHALLENGES AND CELEBRATE SUCCESSES TOGETHER.
THEIR COMBINED TALENTS CREATE SOMETHING UNIQUELY SPECIAL, REFLECTING THEIR PERSONAL AND ARTISTIC GROWTH.

THEIR PROFESSIONAL COLLABORATION LEADS TO A DEEPER PERSONAL CONNECTION. THEY CONFRONT AND NAVIGATE THEIR EVOLVING FEELINGS FOR EACH OTHER. THE DEVELOPMENT OF THEIR RELATIONSHIP ADDS A NEW LAYER TO THEIR CREATIVE WORK AND PERSONAL LIVES.

ELLA AND LUCAS CELEBRATE THEIR ACHIEVEMENTS AND THE STRENGTH OF THEIR PARTNERSHIP. THEIR COLLABORATION IS A TESTAMENT TO THEIR GROWTH AND MUTUAL SUPPORT.

Chapter 8: The Symphony of Stars ♡

ELLA AND LUCAS PRESENT THEIR COLLABORATIVE WORK IN A GRAND PERFORMANCE, SHOWCASING THE CULMINATION OF THEIR CREATIVE JOURNEY.
THE TOWN'S POSITIVE REACTION HIGHLIGHTS THE IMPACT OF THEIR COLLABORATION AND THE CONNECTION THEY'VE ESTABLISHED WITH THE COMMUNITY.

ELLA AND LUCAS DISCUSS THEIR PLANS FOR THE FUTURE, BOTH PROFESSIONALLY AND PERSONALLY. THEIR SHARED EXPERIENCES HAVE LAID THE FOUNDATION FOR CONTINUED SUCCESS AND HAPPINESS.

THE CHAPTER
CLOSES WITH A
SENSE OF
FULFILLMENT AND
HOPE. ELLA AND
LUCAS LOOK
FORWARD TO
THEIR FUTURE
WITH OPTIMISM,
EMBRACING THE
NEW
OPPORTUNITIES
THAT AWAIT
THEM.

the

EnD